In Sunshine and In Shadow

The Complete Poetic Works of
Dennis W. Carroll

Paraline Publishing

Cover photo by Dennis W. Carroll
Cover design by Brandon Hudgens
Book design by Brandon Hudgens

ISBN: 978-0-9898020-2-4
First Printing: January 2014

Eldorado

Gaily bedight,
A gallant knight,
In sunshine and in shadow,
Had journeyed long,
Singing a song,
In search of Eldorado.

But he grew old-
This knight so bold-
And o'er his heart a shadow
Fell as he found
No spot of ground
That looked like Eldorado.

And, as his strength
Failed him at length,
He met a pilgrim shadow-
"Shadow," said he,
"Where can it be-
This land of Eldorado?"

"Over the Mountains
Of the Moon,
Down the Valley of the Shadow,
Ride, boldly ride,"
The shade replied-
"If you seek for Eldorado!"

- Edgar Allan Poe

Forward

Poetry, like all works of art, is conceived in the mind's eye and is bound only by the heart and soul from which it is born. What amazes me about it is the fact that it is a look through the eyes of another and their point of view. It is also a product of life and our experiences and this is the essence of life itself, for our experiences shape us in so many ways into the people that we are to become and are always becoming. True poetry is almost a living thing sometimes, just like life and us, it has a rhythm and it has its meaning. It is the favorite child of writers, for it helps any good wordsmith to paint their picture for you with words, instead Of brush and oils. The words are life captured and the words are yours and mine to keep…

As the poet says:

Still waters run deep....
Their secrets to keep....
It will surely not suffice .....
To never look once....
but always, look twice.....

- Dennis W. Carroll

Contents

Introduction

Since my childhood there has been one writer who has captured my imagination as no other and that is the master wordsmith Edgar Allan Poe. No one could reach out and touch the darkness like Poe and let you feel it too. I have read all the masters from Shakespeare to Stoker (who by the way wrote one of the best books ever written <u>Dracula</u>) from H.G. Welles to Arthur Conan Doyle to Mary Wollstonecraft Shelly (another great book <u>Frankenstein</u>) and the list goes on and on....As Newton said "I have seen farther only because I have stood on the shoulders of giants". Well these writers and others like them have been my giants and on their shoulders I have known other lands and worlds which I couldn't have otherwise...so to you Mr. Poe and the other masters who gave me so much enjoyment and inspiration…I dedicate this humble book and I raise my glass, to you all.

The Story Teller

Let me awaken the memory,
Of the days of old…
When time was free,
And the sun was gold…
When the shadows were as dark,
As the tales that were told.
By the light of the fire,
When the night winds grew cold…

Then late in midnight's lonely hour,
When the Face of the moon is pale.
Gather closer to the fire,
And listen well…
Hold fast to the words,
And break not their spell.
For there are legends left to speak of,
And stories…still to tell…

The Noble Cause

Of all that is noble to be done,
Before one dies…
Is to tell what you have seen,
Through, others eyes…

To leave behind a little,
Of what you've known…
So that others need not walk,
Into the future, alone…

Children of the Dragon

Not all snakes crawl on the ground.....
Some like people walk around....
Their bite is deadly so beware....
the children of the dragon never play fair....
Keep an eye on the shadows stay out of the shade.....
and wherever you walk keep a hand on your blade....
Never forget, after you cut off a snakes head...
The serpent can still bite, even after its dead.....

Ghosts of a Future Lost

I have tasted love's bitter wine,
And I have paid a deadly cost.
Memories of what could have been mine,
Are now the ghosts of a future lost…

Deep in the shadows of this regret,
I linger in this desolate place.
If alas my heart could only forget,
The memory of your sweet embrace…

But it seems that I must carry on,
Against a destiny that is not mine.
Through this vale dark and unknown,
Far beyond any reason or rhyme…

The winds of time so soon will blow,
Over these bones covered with frost.
I will forever haunt the halls of woe,
With the ghosts of a future lost…

Deal With the Devil

Don't ever make a deal,
That's not on the level,
And whatever you do,
Never shake hands with the Devil…

He will start with a compromise,
It will feel good to give in.
But it's all a pack of lies,
In a race you can't win…

The Devil never plays fair…
Never follows any rules…
If you play with him beware…
It's always a game of fools…

He is good at what he does,
He's a master of deceit.
And to deal with the Devil
Is ruin and defeat…

Isle of the Dead

To this city of marble, I have been lead…
To this silent isle of ruin and rubble.
I fear not the places, of the dead,
Only the living, are given to trouble…

Here the dead lie quietly sleeping,
Waiting for a trumpet sound…
Here the dead, their vigil keeping,
Neath the mossy, moonlit ground…

I seek not the voices, of the dead,
But I know the secrets of their stones.
Breath has gone, and blood has bled,
All that is left, is the dust of bones…

But far past this grey, granite cold,
Far beyond this world of sod.
Lives lived and stories told,
Will live on forever, in the heart of God…

Dance With the Devil

Mama told her it just wasn't right
It was time for prayers and a candle to light
Serena's smile like her dress was bright,
As she headed out for the dance that night

Dance like the Devil,
On Sunday night.
Dance like the Devil,
When you know it ain't right.
Dance like the Devil,
Till the break of day.
Dance like the Devil,
While the demons play.

Religion ain't much when you want something more,
The tall dark stranger met her out on the floor,
As he took her in his arms she seemed in a trance,
She looked deep into his eyes as they began to dance.
Faster and faster they moved to the beat,
She knew something was wrong by the look of his feet.
He held her with blazing eyes of fire,
As she gave herself over to dark desire…

You can dance with the Devil,
When you know it ain't right.
Dance with the Devil,
And be lost in the night.
The luck of the Devil never runs that long,
You can only dance with the Devil,
Till the end of the song...

As the crowd watched just before dawn,
A terrible shriek was heard and then it was gone.
A flash of fire and horrible smoke,
The crowd screamed and then they broke.
All they found was a burned piece of Serena's dress,
When your date is the Devil, you go down like the rest…

Dance with the Devil,
In the pale moonlight.
Dance with the Devil,
When you know it ain't right.
Dance with the Devil,
Till the break of day.
But when you dance with the Devil,
There'll be the Devil to pay…
There's always…the Devil to pay…

The Fairest Rose

In the hall of years dear lady,
There is a place where you dwell.
Where our love is forever a thing of legend,
The fairest of stories still to tell.

A thousand swords cannot sunder,
In death and time we will not part.
For our love was the finest flower,
That ever bloomed in the human heart.

There was a place of happiness,
The essence of love divine.
Where I once held you in my arms,
And knew that you were mine.

You have taken the better part of me,
But it was yours from the very start.
And now throughout the ages of eternity,
We two are one to never part.

Oh fairest rose that ever was,
Beyond the veil you wait for me.
Soon the tides of time once more will turn,
At last to set our love forever free…

The Road Unseen

Beyond the shadows of this life,
Beyond the darkness and the green...
The shade of another world is waiting,
Down, a road unseen...

This unknown land is always with us,
Just at the edge of our sight…
Some have the courage to go there,
Fearing not, to face the night…

Far past the boundaries of life and death,
Of what is real and what is dream…
The answers are waiting for us,
Somewhere down, this road unseen…

So let us go once more my friend,
To where the mysteries may gleam,
Beyond the light, into tomorrow,
Down, the road unseen...

He'll Come Knocking at Your Door

In the deepening of the twilight,
Where bitter breezes moan and blow.
Angels of mercy will flee in fright.
From a fate that none should know…

Then he'll come knocking at your door,
He will come for all you hold most dear.
Only then to give you so much more.
Of all that you…will come to fear…

In the gathering darkness of this night,
When shadows dare to walk the land.
All hope will fade with the dying light,
And love will lose its last command…

Then he'll come knocking at your door,
And your soul will pay the cost.
He will take what no one can restore,
And you will be…Forever Lost…

Hope

The human heart, much hope can render...
Though time and pain, can be its foe.
As through the years, hard and tender...
We watch the tides of life, ebb and flow.

But there is a master, over all...
By who's hand, he guides our way.
And beyond, the darkest nightfall...
He gives us hope, for a brighter day.

Then in the time, of trial and sorrow...
When it seems the heart, must surely fail.
Hold fast to that, bright tomorrow...
Where the love of God, will prevail.

Winter of the Heart

The birds have all vanished from the trees,
And autumn's days are almost gone…
Summer lives only in memories,
And now, I face winter all alone…

Wild flowers bloom here no more,
Beneath the trees so silent and dead…
Where is the one I still long for,
Why do I linger, when life has fled…

But somewhere you go on without knowing,
How really well you have played your part…
To bring about the cold wind now blowing,
In what once was the summer, of my heart…

If I could but taste your lips once more,
Or just simply look upon your face…
If I could forget all that has gone before,
Then I might endure, winter's cold embrace…

But Soon the snow will fall from the sky,
And no trace will be found…
Of the dying leaves that now lie,
Like broken dreams, upon the ground…

For others spring may come their way,
But for me it will never start…
Blue skies remain forever gray.
For those who know, the winter of the heart…
And somewhere you will go on without knowing,
Just how well you have done your part…
To bring about the cold wind now blowing,
Deep, in the icy winter of the heart…

At, This Time of Night

The wind moans as if weeping,
The moon rises, cold and white.
Sidewalks all are sleeping,
At, this time of night.

Moving shadows on the wall,
Things, just out of sight.
Who knows what may come to call,
At, this time of night.

Midnight at the window knocks,
Only darkness, beyond the light.
It might be best to check the locks,
At, this time of night.

Strange noises at the door,
The clutch, of fear so tight.
The evening now offers something more,
At, this time of night.

Terror now seems at hand,
Is this the hour, of your flight?
Or will you make your final stand,
At this time of night.

Will you face your fears unknown,
Will you flee, or will you fight?
But it's a thousand years till dawn,
Here at, this time of night.

Tales of the Dark

By the camp fire's spark,
When the world was new.
They told stories of the dark,
And some legends were true.....

In whispers they told,
Of things best left alone.
Of secrets the shadows hold,
And of horrors unknown...

Deep in your soul they abide,
The tales are still within you.
And somewhere deep down inside,
You know that the stories are true...

What waits in the dark?
Only the light can reveal.
Is it imagination's mark?
Or do you know it now to be real....

Mystery

Mystery you are my sweet mistress,
Why do you always haunt me so?
From the days of golden youth,
You have shown me the way to go…

Dark adventure is your enduring charm,
And fantasy your alluring game.
I have know well your taste for horror,
As well as you have known my name…

Once again you will call for me,
Once more your company I will not forsake.
Together hand in hand to walk,
The dark and shadowed path to take…

The Rising Dark

Beyond what is known there is knowledge and power,
In a place far past what is real and what is dream.....
In the halls of darkness you will stand alone in your hour,
For There will be none there to hear you scream...

Then stand to the light with the star of your faith,
Soon will come the turning of the darkest tide....
For the shadows of shade and of wraith,
Will fall to the one on the angel's side....

But there are some things that walk this Earth,
That were never meant to be here.....
And they have given unnatural birth,
To the dire darkness of our fear.....

Then be always on guard my friend,
At all times and on every hand....
For when the light of each day doth end,
Then the shadows of night will rule the land....

So heed the power of the rising dark,
Do not let the worst of evil seek your side....
The heart of your soul is its final mark,
For where there is no light, only darkness will abide....

Something Dreadful

Where the shades will bend and twist,
With the kiss of the night's cold wind,
Your fears will be there to insist,
That you have come to your safety's end.

Then along the dark and shadowed pathway,
Always keep this thought in mind,
That something truly dreadful,
May be coming up, BEHIND…

The Other Side of Midnight

Beyond the sunlit world,
Past all that we know and see…
A darker fate may there await,
Adventurers like you and me...

By chance some here are drawn,
Long after the dying of the light...
To a place where nightmares race,
On the other side of midnight...

Where lurks a rising terror,
Just beyond the human view...
And ghosts of what you dread the most,
May alas become so true...

Here the bravest heart may fail,
Where the sum of all fear is found...
And courage taken may be forsaken,
Upon this dark and unknown ground...

Then beware the shadows as you run,
Through the darkening of the twilight...
For who knows what may wait for you,
On the other side of midnight...

A Dark Wind Blowing

When dogs bay, at a fretful moon,
That's clothed in clouds ragged and torn.
When night-birds suddenly, cease their tune,
Long before, the break of morn...

When children, in restless sleep,
As if to an unheard call.
Awake from frightening, nightmares deep,
To find they have not ended, after all...

When things are not, what they seem,
And darkness gathers all around.
When life becomes, like a dim dark dream,
And you walk on strange, unknown ground...

Then be on guard, at every hand,
In your coming and in your going.
For the shadows that will fall to cover the land,
Are the shades, of a dark wind blowing…

Ghost

For fifteen short years I knew,
What heaven on earth could be…
But Now a sad fate untrue,
Has robbed me of you,
Now the shadows of hell
Follow me…

In what should be my happiest hour,
I lose my smile as I turn away.
My thoughts go to your bower,
Where you hold the flower,
I gave you on your burial day…

You were far past my dreams,
You were better than an angel could be,
But the end it seems,
Doesn't justify the means,
For when you died it took the best part of me…

The vow we took is still good,
I still wear this ring that you see,
Nothing my dear wife ever would,
Come between us if it could,
For I'm still married to the sweet ghost of your memory…

As the sun sets each weary day
I spend the haunted hours in walking this floor,
Waiting for the darkness that will stray,
And that shadows that hold sway,
In the dreams when you will come to me once more…

We will dance again together my dear,
For tonight dark death is our host…
I will hold you so near,
And whisper in your sweet ear,
That it is you who dances with a ghost…

Angel Eyes

In the dark streets of the city,
Where i walk this lonely pace.
Lost in the crowds that know no pity,
I look for you in every woman's face.

These dire days have brought me here,
To walk this world without you.
It seems that my most dreaded fear,
Has alas... become so true.

But your angel eyes are calling me,
Across the dark winds of this night.
Those angel eyes are drawing me,
From the darkness to the light.

For in your dark green angel eyes.
I have seen a love that never dies...

Deep in the watches of the night,
I will long to hold you once again.
But death has won this bitter fight,
All is lost that might have been.

Our golden dream is gone at last,
All the bright lights now fade to blue.
The hope of tomorrow is lost to the past,
The final road I now travel leads only to you.

For your angel eyes are calling me,
Across the dark winds of this night.
Your sweet angel eyes are drawing me,
From the darkness to the light.
For in your dark green angel eyes...
I have found a love, that never dies...
I have known a love...that never dies...

Dark Angel

I want to die standing up on my own…
For death and I have met before.
Then let his bloody blade cut to the bone,
For the spirit will still rise once more…

Your dark throne stands no longer,
Scales of justice pay the cost.
Be not proud you are not stronger,
For the final battle you have lost…

Black angel of the dark wings,
Your victory at last is gone.
With the solemn bell that rings,
The last funeral will be your own…

Shed not for me your lying tears,
Nor show to me your baleful eye.
For when we are gone with the dust of years,
It is the spirit that will not die…

So from the grave there is no surrender,
It does not end in the blood and strife.
A stone is left there to remember,
That here from death rises…eternal life.

Ghost Wolf

Somewhere between the worlds,
A spirit shadow stalks......
In the darkness of the night,
The white ghost wolf walks.....

Guardian of the land and its people,
The glory of days gone by....
He is a Son of the great spirit,
From the tribe of the sky.....

Ghost wolf have you lost your place?
With the children of the moon....
Once among us but found no more,
Are you gone so soon?

They dance to bring you back,
For days gone by they yearn....
But will we see your spirit again?
When shadows of the night, return.....

Deo Favente Resurgam

(With God's Favor I Will Rise Again)

In the blackest night,
And in the darkest hour.
The Lord will be my light,
My refuge and my tower…

In the days of my sorrow,
Like a storm driven bird.
I am given hope for tomorrow,
By the promise of his word…

From where I now stand,
I shall not be forsaken.
From his unfailing hand,
I cannot be taken…

What foe can be my enemy?
What evil can abide?
For mine is the victory,
With The Lord at my side…

If I must fall to the dust,
Then at the end I will begin.
In this I will forever trust,
That with his favor, I will rise again…

Dark River

What few days now are left,
Time will most surely betray.
And the hours that are measured in depth,
Will be the years gone down to decay...

Lost ever far beyond recall,
Are the chances forever flown?
Soon the fortunes of fate will fall,
Where the ashes of the past are blown...

Look not to the walls that have held,
Against the night as dark as coal.
For it is not the light that has failed,
When you have dared to forsake your soul...

Then death in his robes of sorrow,
Will find you waiting by the door.
Then gone are the hopes of tomorrow,
Fled are the dreams that are no more...

Now to face that dark and lonely river,
To stand before the eternal tide.
But beyond the waves that run forever,
Waits a light upon...the other side...

Left Behind

I woke this morning with my pillow in my arms,
For a minute I thought it was you.
I look at this big empty bed and wonder,
Do you miss our love so true?

Do you miss the warmth in the darkness?
Now that you've found someone new.
Though time and the years stand between us,
Deep down I'll be longing for you…

I'll be yearning for your sweet softness,
The happiness that was your embrace.
But the time that was ours is gone now,
The future without you to face…

Deep in the night will you remember?
Will I ever again cross your mind?
Or will you awake some morning,
With no trace of me left behind…

So many bridges burned and fallen,
The path we can never retrace.
Broken dreams beyond all repair,
Have left us here in this place…

Now your journey will continue,
With hope that the miles will be kind.
But you will walk into the years before you,
With no thought of the one left behind…

Death of the Quartermoon

(The Legend of the Ship in the Sand)

Her flag was a skull and crossbones,
She never knew how to fight fair.
In her holds she had a great treasure,
Her destination was an unknown lair.

Somewhere back in the mists of time,
She was overtaken by a strange destiny.
To an even stranger grave,
She was blown in from the sea.

Far from the home that she knew,
Locked in forever by land.
For the time of her remaining,
She is given to a sea of sand.

Some swear to have seen her,
When desert sandstorms blow in the night.
With rotted sails and rusted cannons,
She still stands ready to fight.

For some she is a legend of lost treasure,
For others a mirage at noon.
Far from the coast of the Carolinas,
Flies the ghost of the quartermoon........

Dark Dragons of the Heart

Dark dragons of the heart,
Are a danger to the soul.
For they can rip your world apart,
And they can take a deadly toll.

They have an eye for disaster,
As they await unwary prey.
They can make themselves your master,
Until the final hour of your last day.

They are the bane of your existence,
Seeking only to make you their own.
To take you far beyond the distance,
And turn your heart into stone.

In the world they roar and thunder,
And they feed on sin so well.
They will tear your hopes asunder,
And make your life a living hell.

Dark dragons wait in every heart,
They are evil as black as coal.
Self destruction is their perfected art,
For they are the darkest shadows of your soul...

Blood and Roses

Blood and roses,
This is what the thorns have done.
Life strangely proposes,
That you take your chances on the run...

By sword or knife,
There are wounds that run far too deep.
Life requires life,
For the dreams that shall never sleep...

Hear destiny's laugh,
Where blows this sad and lonely wind.
For the bitter half,
We will now pursue it to this end...

Lost in the haze,
All hope of safety too soon is gone.
At the end of our days,
We will come to face our maker all alone...

Blood and roses,
The hungry need for love will never lie.
One only supposes,
That for this we will live or die…

Phantom Paradise

The tides of love may ebb and flow,
Without rules it will never play nice.
So soon it all will turn to woe,
For fools in a phantom paradise.

Where is that love you had for me,
Where is your heart so true.
Was I so blind i could not see,
Was I to blame or was it you.

Love gone down without a fight,
To a less than noble death.
Now comes the fading of its light,
Now to await the final breath.

Do you know now or even care,
For you have rolled the playing dice.
So ends this sad love affair,
Lost to a phantom paradise...

The Starry Sea

For one to gaze up at night,
Upon the sky's vast starry sea.
Beyond the darkness and the light,
Is to look into the face of eternity...

I have seen far into forever,
Far past the dust of the stars.
To where the spirit must endeavor,
And where the soul will know no bars...

For in the house of tomorrow,
Our children will come to wait.
Beyond the triumph and the sorrow,
To face at last their golden fate...

Onward to the blackness of space,
Where time itself at last will bend.
To the true home of the human race,
And to the dream that has no end...

Lost In the Shadows

Lost in the shadows,
We will play our part.
Lost in the shadows,
To the darkness of the heart...

I see the need in your eyes,
What the body can never forget.
I feel my blood begin to rise,
As we cast aside all regret...

Lost in the shadows,
Lost to these dreams.
Lost in the shadows,
Nothing is ever what it seems...

The night will be what it must,
Love and lust are in our power.
Tomorrow may go down to dust,
Tonight we live within this hour...

Lost in the shadows,
Far beyond the light.
Lost in the shadows,
Lost forever in this night...

Hope of the Heart

How can a man live with,
The bitter taste of love denied?
When it seems, his dreams are gone,
And hope of the heart, has died…

But you are what I long for,
You are the quest of a lonely heart.
The end of all of my desires,
And the beginning, of their start…

For all things and everything,
I can see in your sweet eyes.
The answered longing of all the years,
Dwells there, in disguise…

You are the dream that I pursue,
For which i dare to chance.
The dream that is always before me,
That holds me ever, in its trance…

You can make me or break me,
With a glance of your bright eye.
But for your charms I would live,
And in your arms, I would die.....

For how could a man die better,
Than for the taste of love denied.
And how could he face eternity,
With such a dream, untried.....

The Song of Spring

As the stars wink out, one by one,
Morning takes her walk among the trees.
The song of the birds greet the sun,
And the dawn is kissed by the rising breeze.

Another day is given as a gift,
Of beauty and wonder at every hand.
For the seeds of summer soon will drift,
And renew its promise to the land.

The dead of winter now is past,
Spring comes with flowers in her hair.
She shakes her slumber at long last,
Her song of life, once more to share.

The Far Side of Forever

Sweet, sweet surrender, to love so tender,
Given up to passion's flame...
Nights to remember, what the heart can render,
For true love now has a name...

In your arms to find, sanctuary and peace of mind,
From the weary world without...
Love is a haven kind, with vows that ever bind,
Beyond the shadow of any doubt...

Two together as one, a dream never to be undone,
This is the force of our endeavor...
With this desire won, the lines of our love will run,
To the far side of forever...

Demon Wind

There's a demon wind blowing,
Through the land tonight...
And the darkness now is growing,
Where once was only light...

Down a dark and empty street,
Where the rolling fog has thinned.
Star-crossed lovers here will meet,
Despite this evil wind...

In a world of black and white,
There are shadows that have no end.
Who will pay the price tonight?
Lost in this demon wind...

Beneath a blood red moon,
Dying dreams scream in the night.
One by one they meet their doom,
All to fall within their flight...

In the shadows without,
Strange angels now descend.
And devils are all about,
In the drafts of an unholy wind...

In a world of black and white,
There are shadows end to end.
Far from the hope of any light,
Blows this demon wind...

Hold fast to your love,
And desires of the heart.
When dark winds sound above,
Then comes the hour to depart...

In the night now falling,
Listen not my friend.
To the voices that are calling,
From out that wicked wind...

In a world of black and white,
There are shadows without end.
And somewhere in the night,
Blows a demon wind...

Haunted House

In the night so dark, the air was strange.
The wind that blew, across the grange.
Stirred the branches of the willow,
Whispered past, the silvered window...

A house hides here, from the coming gale.
If it could speak, what stories would it tell.
Would it talk of things that remain unknown?
Of murder at midnight and screams at dawn.
Of spirits that walk, its blood stained floor,
Doomed here to stay, forever more...

Against the wind and the storm,
Here to stand, all alone.
Forsaken and forlorn,
You who once, were a home.

Now only the memories remain,
With their legacy of dust.
Where alas, time and pain,
Have betrayed your trust...

So I leave you, to your sad and lonely fate.
Too soon to come, or perhaps at last, too late.

Haunted thing of wood and stone,
I have found only in you, ghosts of my own...

The Lateness of the Hour

Heed now the rising of the tide,
In these days of dark and deadly fate...
See by the shadows on every side,
That the hour now...is growing late...

The son of darkness will soon arise,
To offer hope and promises to keep...
But he alas can speak only in lies,
To give the nations...just cause to weep...

Souls lost forever to despair,
Fallen angels show their true face...
They will lead so many to the snare,
Of the devil's doomed...and deceitful race...

Come now to the side of the light,
To the truth of God already known...
His star still ever shines so bright,
To show the path...that will lead to home...

Time is bound by destiny's hand,
Mark now the hour that is so late...
Battle lines are drawn for the final stand,
To win or lose the prize...of heaven's gate...

Home from the Sea

Only seabirds now mark the place,
Here upon this lonely golden shore...
Where the tides, never cease,
And the waves sparkle, sparkle ever more...

My watch here is not forsaken,
To where the sea meets the sky...
I look ever to, it's blue edge,
Where a dream waits, to catch my eye...

For I know his ship is coming,
And he will find me waiting here...
With all the love, my heart can give,
To hold again the one, I love so dear...

Through the storms of the ocean to wander,
Nothing will keep him from this bay...
And a woman's heart, that has the magic,
To make the roaming, spirit stay...

I can see the stars through his sails,
And the ghosts of his flags flying free...
From out of all, the lost years,
He at last, has come for me...

Only eternity now will mark the place,

As we sail from this golden shore...

Beyond the tides, that never cease,

And the waves that sparkle, sparkle ever more...

The Hunter's Moon

In the paths of light and shadow,
Beyond the boundaries of night and noon,
There are those who must always answer,
The call of the Hunter's Moon...

The warmth is that much better,
Once that you have known the chill,
And if you have seen the face of darkness,
Then the light will be sweeter still...

For deep in the gathering shadows,
Where night winds play their tune,
Who knows what may walk in the evening,
By the light of the Hunter's Moon...

Hold fast to what you deem most dear,
Take care to guard your very soul,
For the darkness may overtake you,
Before the bells of midnight toll...

There will come a time to fight or flee,
Where your destiny may find you soon,
Along some pale and unknown pathway,
In the light of the Hunter's Moon...

Once This Way I Came

As wasted years one by one must fall,
I find I have myself only to blame.
Lost are the memories that never recall
That once upon a time, this way I came...

Thus death will find me here alone,
The fairest day, must lose its sun.
And when the years at last are gone,
Nothing then, can ever be undone...

So I will slip past this earthly scene,
Beyond all of life's hope and fear.
To leave the final slate wiped clean,
As if that I, were never here...

Then weep no tears for what cannot be,
And leave no flowers in my name.
For only these words are left to see,
To show that once, this way I came...

The Road Unknown

Throughout our lives we roam,
Guided by an unseen hand.
Down a road unknown,
To an undiscovered land.

Here, we meet once more,
Upon this long and winding way.
To see what else life has in store,
To follow the road, come what may.

Far from points, south and north,
Far, far, from the lights of home.
Some are born to adventure forth,
Down this road unknown.

Somewhere there sounds a trumpet call,
That you and I cannot deny.
And even as the silver echoes fall,
We chase them still, until we die.

Now once again, it is time to go,
Where few others, before have gone.
Beyond the sunshine and the shadow,
Waits...the road unknown…

The Fields of November

Deep in these days we know,
There will come a time to remember.
Amid the cold winds that blow,
Over the barren fields of November...

Like the ashes of a long ago fire,
Where no embers now remain.
Happiness from this life will retire,
For nothing ever can stay the same...

Destiny has put out the candle,
And life now must ever render.
Too much time and pain to handle,
In these forsaken fields of November...

The spirits of dead memories,
Return again upon this night.
With hands that never set you free,
Even after darkness turns to light...

If only the lonely human heart,
Could forget all it must remember.
Gone like nature's forgotten part,
In the windswept fields of November...

The Devil Undone

Dark days, are fast upon us,
Blood now will freely run...
But we must do what we must,
To see that the Devil, is undone...

Now is the time, of all or nothing,
Now to take the final stand...
Where darkness will meet the light,
There to wait, with sword in hand...

No more lies, no more deception,
The day of destiny has come...
When the pure of heart will finally see,
The Devil at last, undone...

Queen of the Night

I have found no greater love than this,
My beautiful goddess of delight.
I long ever for the bliss, of your pale kiss,
My fair haired queen of the night...

Lost in the soft embrace of your arms,
Two hearts forever to be as one.
For time will never harm, your enduring charms,
When all at last is said and done...

In your eyes i have seen a love so true,
With a passion that knows no bars.
You have reached far into, the heavens blue,
And clothed yourself with stars...

My huntress stalks the sky's dark stair,
Where night-birds will take to wing.
She comes to dare, the den of the lion's lair,
And put her arrow to its string...

Then bend your bow and let loose your dart,
I fall to your bright rising light.
Now heart to heart, paradise here will start,
My sweet noble queen of the night...

Midnight Rain

On this stormy windswept night,
I recall a dream that died in vain.
I remember your sweet eyes so bright,
And the tears you gave, to the midnight rain...

I throw open the windows wide,
And I call your name in the wind.
But memories keep the hurt alive inside,
And they will haunt me, to the bitter end...

Somewhere in this broken heart,
Once more I must face the pain.
Our goodbyes were only the start,
Of a love lost, to the midnight rain...

The dark is filled with ghosts tonight,
Where the shadows twist and bend,
They are waiting just beyond the light,
On this night, that has no end...

Deep in the darkest of my hours,
Even in dreams I cannot be free,
I know the hunger for what was ours,
And for what now, will never be...

In the halls of a lonely heart,
I will surrender to this pain.
To mourn a love lost from the start,
Lost like tears, in the midnight rain...

Lost In the Moment

Lost in the beauty, of the moment,
When I first saw heaven in your eyes.
I fell to love's every component,
With a feeling far greater, than the skies...

Deep in the longing, of the lonely,
There is a need for love so true.
In your arms I have found this only,
And now I need, only you...

Take my heart, then hand in hand,
We will walk throughout this life.
Together we will make our stand,
Against the time, of storms and strife...

Mere words my darling, fail to convey,
The essence of a love so good and bright.
For the human heart can never say,
That which poets, cannot write...

Lost Dreams

As the light of life swiftly passes,
Then the days of youth must surely die,
And like pride, that has turned to ashes,
Love can forsake you by and by...

In my heart I long for yesterday,
Where still you live in my memory's glow,
Long before it seems, that I lost my way,
In the shadowed years of long ago...

Now only the lonely tears remain,
The echo of dreams that have gone to dust,
In this sad gray city, they fall like rain,
To mourn a legacy of regret and rust...

Dreams and days now forever lost,
The ghosts of recollections left behind,
Where a star-crossed love, has paid the cost,
To haunt the dark streets of the mind...

Somewhere In the Night

Memories whisper to me,
In the cold night winds that blow.
They say that I have lost forever,
The girl that I love so....

In the rain, the shadows fall,
From darkness into light.
And the storms of life are gathering,
Somewhere in the night…

Somewhere in the night,
There is shelter from the storm.
Eyes that call to me,
And lips so soft and warm…

Somewhere lovers meet,
Somewhere hearts are light.
But loneliness will always call,
Somewhere in the night…

Long I linger in the shadows,
With the darkness and the rain.
All that's left are the memories,
And an ever present pain…

Somewhere do you lie alone?
When there are arms to hold you tight.
And a heart that still longs for you,
Somewhere in the night…

Somewhere in the night,
In the winds of the storm.
The memories will wait for me,
Where the pain is born…

Somewhere lovers meet,
Somewhere hearts are light.
But tears will always fall,
Somewhere in the night…

Forgotten Ruins

If I were a fortress, I would lie in ruins,
For there is no light of life left in me.
Alone I wait, forsaken and desolate,
A shell is all that there is to see…

The weeds of lost love and its memories,
Here grow to block out the sun.
And a cold wind blows, through the holes,
Of what time and pain have done…

The birds of quiet despair and loneliness,
Here nest to sing their sad refrain.
To never know at length, of the strength,
That has fled forever from this domain...

So the story is told after all,
And the ruins remain as a reminder to stand,
For every wall, that did sadly fall,
Was brought down, by a woman's hand…

Lines In the Sand

Here in this time where I now stand,
To watch the waves upon life's shore.
I ponder these lines written in the sand,
Soon lost to the ages forevermore...

Will the legacy that I leave behind,
Be but words whispered into the wind.
And all the ties I've tried to bind,
Will they be for nothing in the end...

Perhaps the truths that I have spoken,
Will be the only gift I have to give.
When at last the golden bowl is broken,
They alone will be left to live...

Then the lines found written in the sand,
Upon this shore that you will trod.
Are really written by a much greater hand,
With words found only in the heart of god...

Song of the Shadows

Pieces are set for the final game,
That I have no will left to play.
Returning nightmares remain the same,
Even in the light of day…

I have come to a place where night is king,
And deep in the shadow of its heart.
Darkness has become a living thing,
Demanding more than an equal part.

The lines are drawn here to this end,
The circle at last is complete.
And in the blast of life's icy wind,
I hear the whispers of a deadly deceit.

Bright dreams are all fled and lost,
Where hope has followed after.
And courage withers in the burning frost,
Of a cold and mocking laughter.

Now into this dim and darkened land,
I have wandered far for a light to see.
But there is only darkness at every hand,
For now the shadows, belong to me…

Things Unseen

There is far more to this life,
More to this world of blue and green,
And in the night of danger and strife,
Move the forces, that are unseen...

For there is a darker side of day,
That is just beyond the human eye,
And they say it is best not to stray,
To where the light, goes to die...

Beware the journey that you make,
If you must walk the shadows alone,
For there are things that seek to take,
The very soul, you call your own...

Then be on guard as on you go,
To where the shades are heard to keen,
For in the dark of every shadow,
May wait the things, that are unseen...

Two Into One

Far, far, beyond forever,
Through the ages of endless time.
The years of eternity, will not sever,
The words written, upon this line.

Two into one, to never part,
For I am yours and you are mine.
By the power, of the human heart,
Our two fates, will intertwine.

For in your eyes, I have seen tomorrow,
There to share a true love divine.
As we journey past, this vale of sorrow,
To where the stars, forever shine.

Then take my hand and take my heart,
I am yours and you are mine.
Two into one, to never part,
For love will conquer, death and time…

The Fate of Science

Man of science, where is your heart,
Where is the measure of the soul...
Was your quest flawed from the start,
Has it taken now a deadly toll...

Oh science where is your hope now gone,
Has your faith sadly lost its place...
Will it fall before the dark unknown,
To at last betray the human race...

Children of science from truth to stray,
Your trust in tomorrow is now forsaken...
From the path of God you have gone away,
And now in sorrow your time is taken...

Oh science, where is your heart,
Where is the measure of the whole...
You failed to weigh the unseen part,
And that is where, you lost your soul...

The Lonely Road

I walk down this lonely road,
And I walk it all alone.
It's the only thing I know,
To travel on, without a home.

The way goes on before me,
My shadow only by my side.
Looking for somewhere to be,
Without a dream, to be my guide.

Like words on a forgotten line,
In a book that will never be read.
Lost is the hope that once was mine,
Left to the sorrow, of things unsaid.

So, on I go through the shadows,
Of the cold and empty night.
Following the road as on it goes,
Searching ever, for the light.

Have I dearly paid the cost,
Of my life's weary load?
Only to be hopelessly forever lost,
Somewhere down, this lonely road...

To The Rose

The beautiful rose they say,
Is the fairest of all the flowers...
She crowns the sun of every day,
And is the queen, of all her hours...

Holding court by the garden wall,
She wins the heart of all who see...
But her beauty alas will only recall,
The sad memory, that I carry with me...

For when the blossoms bloom in time,
I will think of a place far away.
And of a red rose that is hers and mine,
It is there my thoughts, will always stray...

To the spot of ground that has my heart,
Where rests the one who holds a single rose...
To the memories that will never depart,
And the love that still, forever grows...

Rising Up From the Dead

There's a lonely, night wind drumming.
In the leaves that rattle, like dry bones.
And in the darkness, there's something coming.
From out among, the gray tombstones.

Haunting memories, of you still bind me.
The ghosts of things, we've left unsaid.
They're coming back, tonight to find me.
They're rising up, rising up, from the dead…

I dread the setting, of the sun.
This nightmare waits, for me still.
No place to hide, nowhere to run.
From spirits rising, rising with the chill.

They say old memories, never die.
Tonight i know it, to be so true.
In the shadows I see, the gleam of your eye.
The only ghosts here, are me and you.

Haunting memories, of you still bind me.
The ghosts of things, we've left unsaid.
They're coming back, tonight to find me.
They're rising up, rising up, from the dead…
Rising up…From the dead…

Grave With Out a Name

Throughout the years of our lives,
As the days march steadily on...
Despite deception and its lies,
We are lead to a truth that stands alone...

Deep in the shadows of the dark,
There is a light that will not fail...
And by the power of its holy mark,
It will prevail against the gates of hell...

Hear it speak now in the quiet halls,
Of the sad and lonely heart...
And when the final darkness falls,
It leaves a comfort that will not depart...

For that which was given is not gone,
The gift of a father's great love...
The star of Bethlehem will still shine on,
Forever from the heavens above...

Against death's cold and darkest bowers,
That blessed hope does now remain...
The heavenly promise that is still ours,
From an empty grave without a name...

The Fires That We Burn

The autumn winds are sighing,
As the leaves, begin to turn.
And another year is slowly dying,
In the fires, that we burn...

But one thing will forever remain,
And that, is my love for you.
It will always be the same,
Never ending, and ever true...

Deep in the heart of December,
In the silence, of the falling snow.
Our love will be an undying ember,
That will never, fail to glow...

It is the promise of the summer's sun,
In the cold of winter's, darkest night.
It will rise to chase the shadows that run,
Before the coming, of the morning light...

Sadly the years are not ours to own,
Too soon the cord, begins to fray.
But life will not end beneath a stone,
For love, will find a way...

Time can be a master cruel,
With it's hard, lessons to learn.
But our love will be the fuel,
Of the fires, that we burn...

Spirits of the Dead

Deep in the darkening shadows,
In the dead hours without light...
The memories will rise again,
With the ghosts of the night...

Oh whispering spirits of the past,
What have I to do with you...
You offer only an open grave,
For a life once so good and true...

But she is gone beyond the veil,
She has left me here instead,
Alone to wander these haunted halls,
With the spirits of the dead...

Far past the pain of yesterday,
Ten thousand years of lost tomorrows...
The endless night will find me here,
Still dressed in this robe of sorrows...

Oh to turn again the wheels of time,
To hold what was mine once more...
But all is lost to the darkness,
And the days that have gone before...

Now to remain far past regret,
With these bones so dark and red...
With the revenant of the forsaken years,
And the spirits of the dead...

She waits

Late of a summer's night,
When the wind is in the trees.
And a full moon hangs high and bright,
Throwing shadows to the breeze.

There will come a scent in the air,
Of roses...All around.
It is then I know that she'll be there,
Without a trace of a sound.

Standing in the silver moon beams,
That linger in her raven hair.
A green eyed shade who haunts my dreams,
Is waiting for me there.

She is waiting for me always,
Calling for me in the night.
Through the ever darkening haze,
Where night birds take to flight.

And when the moon hangs no longer high,
As to the west it faces.
She and I will answer the echoing cry,
Of the lonely windswept places.

Soon the dawn will come to be,

But kind are the fates.

For with the night again she will come to me,

For me alone...she waits…

Empty Rooms

Somewhere in the shadows,
That are cast without light.
Somewhere down a lonesome road,
Upon a dreary night…

A banshee wind is blowing,
Through the valley of the moon.
In the dust the shades are rising,
And they only whisper doom…

Where ends the pathway here,
A house waits with open door.
Its memories are many,
Its glory days are no more....

The wind moans lost and lonely,
Round these walls of pale stone.
This haunted place has weathered,
Many a storm to stand alone…

In its shadowed halls I wander,
With only a candle flame.
That stands against the darkness,
To see what calls my name…

I halt before a darkened mirror,

My destiny has come too soon.

For by this glass I finally see,

That I'm the only ghost here, in this room…

Moonrise

I hear the call of every shadow,
Just beyond the pale moonlight.
Drawn to the darkness I must go,
One of the children of the night...

I go now where I've gone before,
Into the blackness that I must wander.
To feel again the animal roar,
Where body and soul are torn asunder...

To be one again with the night,
Is the spell that holds me still.
And once more by the moon's light,
I will go on the hunt for my kill...

Now to stalk the darker side,
Following ever close behind.
I use the eyes of even tide,
For the prey that I must find...

Free at last I run alone,
Without care and without fear.
The hunger of blood drives me on,
To follow the chase far and near...

Soon in the wind there is a hint,
Of the coming of the dawn,
And I catch the morning scent,
That rises from the wooded lawn...

As star dials turn toward morn,
The night has shown me what can be.
Again I will know nature's scorn,
For once more I must wear humanity...

But the change will always find me,
The beast within is coming soon.
To break the chains that bind me,
With the rising of the moon...

In the House of Forever

There is a place I know,
Where some may go...
It's called the house of forever.
And it has been told,
You will never grow old...
In this house of forever.

But there is a price to be paid,
For those who have strayed...
Into the house of forever.
For as the ages pass by,
Here your sins will not die...
In the house of forever.

Here the dragon is lord,
Of a great demon horde...
In the house of forever.
He rules with a sword of dread,
Where all hope has long ago fled...
From the house of forever.

It's rooms are many and dark,
Here Cain has left his mark...
Upon the house of forever.
It's halls are hungry and red,
Here the living are the dead...
In the house of forever.

Where the fallen have fell,
Just past the shadowed veil...
Stands the house of forever.
Behind its door of sorrows,
Are all the lost tomorrows...
In the house of forever.

Here nightmares live to grow,
And all your dreams turn to woe...
In this house of forever.
Beyond the hope of any light,
Here waits eternal night...
In the house of forever.

Run Into the Night

Beware the clouded days of doom,
Beware the darkness you make your own.
For along the pathway to your tomb,
The seeds of destruction have been sown...

Then you'd best run into the night,
And leave the darkness far behind.
Run to that ever shinning light,
Beyond the shadows of your mind...

Can you hear now that echoing chorus,
Upon a dim and far distant shore.
It tells of hope that has flown before us,
Gone to the dust to rise no more...

But there is a starry way above,
Beyond the road you must walk alone.
To find a much greater love,
And to know a far better home...

So run now into the night,
At last to see no longer blind.
Run ever onward to the light,
And let the darkness fall behind...
And leave the darkness far behind...

The End

I feel now the number of my days,
And in the silence, of the empty night.
I must stand alone as always,
To face the end, just out of sight...

I will have become what I fear the most,
When each day, has a darker cast.
And when every memory has its ghost,
I will know that better, days have passed...

Years spent like half remembered dreams,
Soon forgotten, in the morning light.
But their shadows will return again it seems,
To haunt you night, after lonely night...

Now that I have seen the end to be,
I still struggle on, beneath this load.
Only to find that my destiny,
At last is met, upon this road...

So all my days have come down to this,
Like smoke given, unto the wind.
Lost to the stars that will ever kiss,
The blackness, that has no end...

"Is all that we see or seem, but a dream, within a dream…"

- Edgar Allan Poe

www.ingramcontent.com/pod-product-compliance
Lightning Source LLC
Chambersburg PA
CBHW032113040426
42337CB00040B/360